McCOMB PUBLIC LIBRARY
McCOMB, OHIO

In Memory of

Presented by

UPCYCLING
OUTDOORS

UPCYCLING
OUTDOORS

Max McMurdo

PHOTOGRAPHY BY BRENT DARBY

jacqui
small

Text © Max McMurdo 2018
Design, layout and photography © Quarto Publishing Group plc 2018

First published in 2018 by
Jacqui Small
An Imprint of The Quarto Group
The Old Brewery
6 Blundell St
London N7 9BH, United Kingdom
T (0)20 7700 6700 F (0)20 7700 8066
www.QuartoKnows.com

Publisher: Jacqui Small
Managing Editor: Emma Heyworth-Dunn
Design and Art Direction: Rachel Cross
Commissioning Editor: Joanna Copestick
Editor: Sian Parkhouse
Photographer: Brent Darby
Illustration: Max McMurdo
Production: Maeve Healy

The author has made every attempt to draw attention to safety precautions,
but it is the reader's responsibility to ensure safety practices while carrying
out techniques outlined in this book.

ISBN: 978-1-911127-22-2

A catalogue record for this book is available from the British Library.

2020 2019 2018
10 9 8 7 6 5 4 3 2

Printed in China

Quarto is the authority on a wide range of topics.

Quarto educates, entertains and enriches the lives of
our readers — enthusiasts and lovers of hands-on living.

www.QuartoKnows.com

CONTENTS

FOR THE LOVE OF DESIGN

Welcome to my world: sawdust, sketches and silly ideas that occasionally turn into something rather wonderful, but often remain just a lovely creative dream.

I am told on a regular basis by friends and family that I am too optimistic, that I get carried away by my latest wacky ideas and I get prematurely excited before contracts are even signed. Yes I do all of these things - because it makes me happy! The thought of conceptualizing an idea, researching, developing, making prototypes and finally displaying the finished product in all its glory is what makes me tick.

Design is the most wonderful thing. There are no rights and wrongs, everyone has an opinion and anyone can access it in some form.

As if that wasn't enough, upcycled design has the added benefit that you are rescuing items that were otherwise destined to be destroyed and have potentially saved someone from buying a new, inferior piece of furniture. Combine that with the fact that you are learning new skills and sharing those with like-minded creative individuals and you start to understand why I am so passionate about upcycling.

WHAT IS MY JOB TITLE?

I get asked this a lot and those online drop-down menus never have a suitable option for me! I've been called an entrepreneur due to my successful pitch in the *Dragons' Den* and I do run my own business. But, like most creatives, my motivation is rarely to make money. I like saving items from landfill and I love the story behind my designs. I enjoy inspiring people through social media, presenting TV and writing articles. I find working with my hands therapeutic and there is nothing more satisfying than experimenting with new materials and learning new techniques.

When I started upcycling in 2002 my motivation was primarily to design in an environmentally friendly way, using waste materials and as little energy in the process as possible. Increasingly, I realized that with a limited volume of sales it would be very hard as a manufacturer to impact landfill, especially when you take into account all the mass-produced chipboard furniture being created. My focus therefore has shifted slightly over the years to inspire and educate - encouraging people to consider reuse, repair and upcycling before binning and replacing.

In the last few years I have taken this a step further. I have realized that with a shortage of hands-on educational opportunities, young people who are not traditionally academic can feel disheartened and unmotivated to learn. Skills such as metal fabrication, woodwork and upholstery can provide much-needed opportunities. I have recently been working with homeless charities to utilize upcycling as a means of reskilling, and using it as a motivational tool to improve mental health and confidence while also raising funds for support services.

I never for one moment thought my designs would be interesting enough for TV shows and book writing, but I'm glad they are. It turns out I love designing and making under pressure and being out of my comfort zone. It's hard

enough designing and making items in my workshop, but when you're in someone's house, producing something for them out of the waste items they have in their shed, with only the tools you have with you, that's a challenge - and one I thrive on!

So to answer the question, what is my job title? I would say I am fortunate to be able to design and make innovative items, while trying to help the planet and inspire others to explore their creativity. Try fitting that on a business card!

WHY UPCYCLE OUTDOORS?

At a guess I would say that upcycling in its most raw form probably originated outdoors, not for aesthetic reasons or to create a statement, but out of necessity. I remember vividly my parents using two small repurposed, modified plastic drinks bottles as hoppers to dispense slug repellent, and empty yoghurt pots filled with fat and seeds to feed the birds.

In the '50s and '60s we didn't own lots of shiny possessions, store cards didn't exist and you couldn't just buy furniture and cars on easy credit, so we made do with what we had, repaired it if it broke and looked after it to ensure it lasted.

Gardens have never seen that much design attention. They used to be regarded as places to kick a ball, grow some veg or build a shed to house the lawnmower. Now, however, thanks to ever-increasing house prices, rather than moving, habitants are spilling out of their homes and into outdoor spaces, creating sanctuaries of relaxation, from a courtyard to unwind in after a hard day's work to a balcony to open onto at dinner parties.

If you need even more evidence just look at the current trends in interiors: gold pineapples adorn dining tables, pink flamingos are on fabrics and wallpapers, while cactuses and air plants have never seen so much popularity. Urban jungle is everywhere; bringing the outside in is the current architectural must-have, and biophilic design (the addition of natural materials, textures and increased natural light into an interior - particularly urban spaces) is visible in all the big creative offices.

I feel that, traditionally speaking, products for the garden have been less design-led and more functional and practical. However, that is changing. Gone are the days of outdoor wood preservatives being only available in sludge brown, puddle brown or yuck brown — we are seeing a wonderful array of colourful paints and waxes. Placing items in the garden usually used exclusively inside our homes has also become popular, and this can create a very magical, fairytale look to our outdoor space.

WORKING OUTDOORS

If you are designing an item to be used outdoors there are a number of additional factors you may need to take into account. Exposure to the elements and durability are probably the major factors; whether it's the material you are upcycling or the coating you are selecting, the wind, rain and sun will be doing their utmost to damage your creations.

I love being provocative by taking items out of context, such as the flatpack chipboard coffee table on pages 100—103, which was designed to spend its life indoors. But good outdoor upcycling can also be achieved by simply modifying an object that's already designed to live outdoors. Take the upcycled picnic table on pages 92—95, for example. This was an item that was serving its purpose in a perfectly functional way — that's why these table-and-bench sets are so popular — and it just needed bringing up to date with a little designer twist to give it a little individuality.

Some of the larger items featured in this book may need to be constructed in situ, which brings extra practical considerations,

such as access to electricity for power tools. But a bit of clever repurposing can help out here. The three—door potting shed on pages 50—55, for example, was actually created specifically for people with limited outdoor space — you could very easily carry each component through your house and into your courtyard back garden where it could be assembled. And it's not an issue if you don't have power as by reusing the existing hinges and cutting the board for the shelf with a hand saw, all you would need is a cordless drill and a few hand tools.

One of the most interesting aspects of garden design for me is that residents tend to be braver with their gardens than they are indoors. We do tend to play it safe in our houses, perhaps worried that creating a look that's too personal and niche will have an adverse effect on resale value. However, when it comes to our gardens we don't seem to be so constrained. The use of bright bold colours and quirky planters are wonderful opportunities to express your creativity and impress your dinner party guests.

It's also interesting how the style and aesthetic in a garden can be drastically different from that in the home, although I think some of the most successful garden designs are sympathetic with the surrounding architecture. For example, a natural woven-willow fence or pastel-painted furniture works seamlessly with a country cottage, while sharply angular wood, chrome and metal items and furniture are more suitable for an urban balcony or rooftop garden.

But that doesn't mean you should limit yourself; pushing your boundaries and venturing into alternative styles while learning new techniques and skills is also very important and rewarding. I'm personally a big fan of the rustic, industrial look. Using bright bold colours does not come naturally to me, so creating an item like the dressing table plant display stand on pages 62—65 took a bit more effort, as I knew it simply couldn't

remain unpainted wood in an outdoor setting. But the results made it completely worthwhile.

Selecting the right materials to upcycle outdoors is slightly more tricky, as you have to take into account the effect of the elements — wind, rain and sun are not always your friend! You will have to consider applying paints, waxes, stains, oils or even completely coating a finished item in a weatherproof seal. Over the following pages you will see designs produced from chipboard, timber, metal and fabric, some of which come into contact with flames, are portable, and some of which even illuminate - all in an environment that can be very unforgiving, the great outdoors. As with the best interior design, however, I think it's really important to create a balanced look to your garden that incorporates these different materials, colours and styles.

SCAVENGE LIKE A PRO

I've said it before and I'll say it again, sourcing good waste is the key to successful upcycling. Selecting the right base materials makes the entire process a lot easier and therefore more enjoyable. That said, items of decent secondhand furniture are getting harder to get hold of, as the next generation of waste furniture from the last decade is mainly chipboard.

Until recently I've avoided working with chipboard as it's difficult to cut, sand, glue, screw and just generally do anything with. But I guess I have to face up to the inevitable, as most domestic and commercial furniture is now mass produced, flatpack and price driven. If you are going to source material such as chipboard and use it outdoors, however, you will have to build durability and weatherproofing into your design.

Fortunately, with modern chalk paints you can at least now paint laminated surfaces, and I find that cutting coated chipboard with a router creates a nice clean bevelled edge. In terms of attachments, glues are getting stronger, mechanical fixings like nuts and bolts can work well, and I've even had some success using traditional manufacturing techniques such as dowels and pegs to join such materials.

Architectural salvage yards are great places to source materials for outdoor upcycling. Items such as galvanized troughs, concrete slabs, porcelain tiles, terracotta pots and enamel bathtubs are plentiful and not too pricey. Don't worry if items are a little bit damaged — you can design around the affected areas and actually add a bit of rustic charm.

If you are using materials that are not naturally destined to be used outdoors then you will have to consider treating them. This doesn't mean you have to produce the item and then coat it as an afterthought; you can often design the item to be beautiful and durable to the elements at the same time. Water is often an issue, particularly with planters; a few well-located drainage holes or a plastic liner usually solves the problem.

So all is not lost. Yes, we are going to have to think outside the box and design smarter than ever, but I truly believe with some clever upcycling techniques we can continue saving furniture from landfill, even in this flatpack chipboard era.

IT'S EASIER THAN EVER TO UPCYCLE

The trend toward upcycling is increasing in popularity by the day. Online stores are crammed full of beautifully painted furniture, most interior magazines have pages dedicated to the movements and incredibly upcycling now appears to be influencing the interior design movement. To my mind, it's no coincidence that the last two big trends in interiors — shabby chic and the industrial look — both predominantly feature upcycled products, albeit in very different aesthetics. The current urban jungle theme also combines a variety of green tones borrowed from nature with readily upcycled manufacturing and industrial materials such as copper, timber and steel.

Upcyclers are a wonderfully vocal bunch and usually very happy to share ideas and tips. Social media plays a big part in spreading the message, as does the array of upcycling-based TV shows.

Incredibly, many consumers are now searching out skill-enhancing experiences rather than yet more shiny new products. Commercially speaking, running workshops and offering opportunities to learn new skills are also a great way for any creative to generate revenue.

Innovative new products and materials are also assisting us in successful upcycling, both professionally and at home. These include amazing chalk paints that require less preparation, spray-on vinyl coatings that can be changed with the seasons, adhesives that bond the most unlikely of materials and much more affordable power tools.

THE FUTURE OF UPCYCLING

Let's be honest, when I started upcycling even I didn't truly believe that 15 years on there would be TV shows, events and magazines dedicated to the subject. Who could have believed that people all over the world would be making things from scrap rather than buying new?

I attribute this phenomenon to a number of things. During the economic downturn people were forced to think about their consumer habits and cut back on spending. There is an ever-growing awareness of environmental issues, leading us to reduce personal waste. And finally, as I have mentioned, interior design trends were favourable.

A few years ago, when shabby chic was at its peak, I had a few wobbly moments when I wondered if upcycling had the ability to sustain a long-term business. The distressed look was incredibly fashionable, and furniture painters attacked anything that didn't move. But design was evolving, and I wondered if upcyclers could move with the trends.

Then we saw glimpses of the industrial look becoming popular: exposed metal conduit on brick walls, scaffold board and pallet furniture started appearing in room sets and restaurants. Even rust became the new must-have finish! Initially I thought this was an incredible stroke of luck, as these materials are an upcycler's dream. But then it dawned on me - perhaps upcyclers were actually setting and influencing the interior design trends rather than following them?

Incredibly we are now seeing high street stores selling faux upcycled products. This is a testament to the terrific movement of small creative businesses, working tirelessly in back bedrooms, garages and sheds around the country, attending craft fairs and exhibitions, selling online and ensuring customers are not forced into buying mass-produced generic furniture. Instead they can support a small business by purchasing a unique, handmade product that has been designed and produced with love, passion and emotion.

PLANTERS + CONTAINERS

From plastic pots to terracotta troughs, planters are typically practical items. Fear not, this chapter shows you how it's possible to transform easily sourced, everyday items into beautiful yet functional designs to house your plants. Don't panic if your back garden has limited space — there is something for everyone, from a single pot suspended in copper pipes to an old suitcase. Think colour, texture, innovative finishes and even a few surprises as I experiment with some materials for the very first time.

Planters, like most objects designed to be used outdoors, require careful consideration of the elements. But you have the added challenge of providing good growing conditions for your plants, which means getting the water levels right. Too much and your plants will drown; too little and they will quickly dry out, especially in hanging containers. Either way they end up dead, and that is not a good look! To make sure any excess water drains away, drill a few drainage holes in any container, positioning them at the lowest point where water will gather. Use a gritty mix of compost or potting medium. This will also help with weight issues. Bear in mind wet soil can add considerably to overall load-bearing.

Plants come in all shapes, sizes and colours, and it's important to get the combination right when upcycling outdoors. For some projects I've used softer trailing plants to spill out of the items; others require a more structured, architectural plant to complement the design. Always think about where the plants will be located.

Good plants to think about for your containers are easy-maintenance succulents, such as houseleeks (*Sempervivens*) and sedums — these have great architectural forms and beautiful almost metallic colours. Herbs can be quickly replenished when you've used them up in the kitchen, and offer great foliage, from frothy feathery dill to lushly green basil and soft grey thyme. Ivy is tough as old boots and will soon get established. For summer colour, roses are always a great choice, or the exotic-looking flowers of fuchsia and pelargoniums.

COPPER PLANTER

Copper is quite possibly the most fashionable material of the moment. It looks gorgeous whether in its natural form or highly polished. And even when left outside to age, it will develop a verdigris finish so that it takes on another look altogether. I think the combination of the rustic rope, shiny copper and greenery from the plant looks stunning, and you don't need lots of time to create it or space to position it.

Upcyclers sometimes get nervous when it comes to experimenting with metal as it typically needs power tools to join or cut. Copper pipe, however, is designed to be cut with a manual pipe slice, which cuts the pipe perfectly with just a few turns of the tool and even leaves a smoothly finished edge. It's a fantastic tool that performs its job really well.

Getting your head around the threading assembly process can take a while, but once you've figured it out you can create as many of these beautiful hanging planters as you wish. They also make great gifts, and fold flat if you wish to send them out to friends and family.

ITEMS TO SOURCE:
- *assorted lengths of copper piping*
- *large, empty tin can*
- *rope*

1. MEASURE TIN CAN

USE YOUR CAN AS THE STARTING POINT FOR THE DIMENSIONS OF THE PIPE

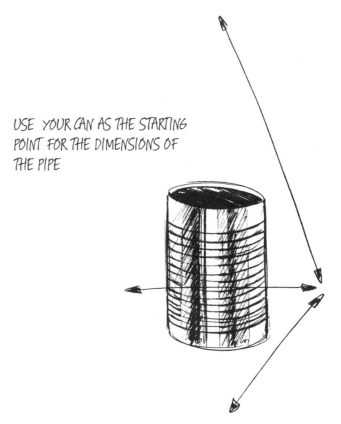

Lay your can on its side, and measure the lengths of copper required. You will need three of each length to give nine pieces in total.

2. CUT PIPE

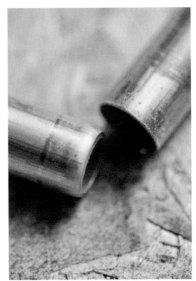

Mark the copper and cut using a pipe cutter. This leaves a nice curved smooth finish on the outside, so just use a small round file to de-burr the inside of the cut edge.

3. CHECK FIT

Assemble the copper pipe pieces around the can in a diamond formation (essentially two pyramids one on top of each other) so you can check you have the correct lengths to form your planter.

Decide where you want your planter to be positioned and how low you want it to hang – this will give you your measurement for the rope. Cut the rope into three equal pieces, but make them longer than required to allow for knotting; you can always cut them down afterwards.

4. CUT ROPE

5. THREAD PIPES

Lay out each piece of rope, then thread on the copper pipes, starting with the short base pieces, then the medium horizontal ones, then the long top pieces.

Tie all three pieces of rope together securely at the bottom with an overhand knot pulled tight.

6. FORM BASE PYRAMID

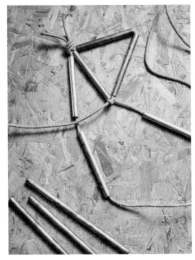

To create the cradle for the pot to sit in, create the smaller bottom pyramid by knotting the ropes together in the gaps between the short and medium pieces as shown, so that the medium pieces sit horizontally and join up end to end.

7. TIE OFF

Make the final knot to secure the base pyramid. You might find it easier to temporarily remove the long pieces of pipe while you pull the knots through tightly.

8. ASSEMBLE TOP PYRAMID

Rethread the three long pipes to form the top section of the planter. Tie a knot in the top and hey presto!

LIVING WALL FROM GUTTERING

When you have limited outdoor space it's great to create as many planting opportunities as you can. Vertical planting, intended to produce the effect of a 'living' wall, has been the hot feature in a lot of great garden design recently, especially for urban yards and patios. This design uses basic plastic guttering, which is really easy to source from any hardware store. It works beautifully for plants that don't require too much soil, such as succulents. This is a really affordable way of creating a living wall that is great to look at but also practical — the whole thing weighs a lot less than alternative living wall structures and can be positioned anywhere, even a balcony or roof terrace.

I have opted for four lengths of guttering, but you can use as many as you wish, cut to length to suit your space. You could, of course, paint the guttering in bright colours, but I was after a sleek contemporary look to complement my houseboat. Grey is also a nice neutral tone to allow the plants to stand out. The combination of the glossy grey plastic, natural rope and the different shades of succulents is incredible.

ITEMS TO SOURCE:
- *plastic gutter pipe*
- *end caps*
- *rope*

1. CUT GUTTERING

Lay out the guttering, measure, mark and cut to the length you want using a hacksaw, holding the piece steady as you do. File the sawn ends smooth with a half-moon file or sandpaper.

2. FIT CAPS

If you need drainage holes drill through the base of each length in several places. Attach some end caps to the guttering.

3. MEASURE AND KNOT ROPES

Measure out enough rope to create a loop for your desired length and then cut two of these lengths using a knife. Tie a knot at the halfway point in each piece of rope – this will sit centrally on the underside of the bottom piece of guttering. Fold the ropes at the central knot. Measure and mark every 25cm (10 inches) and knot the rope at each marked point. Repeat for both ropes.

TIP: Heat the cut ends of the rope with a lighter to seal and prevent fraying.

4. FIX TO BENCH AND CHECK

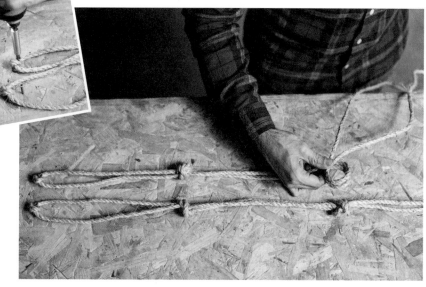

To create tension for the ropes, screw two screws into a workbench and then loop the ropes around them. Check that the knots align on both ropes (so that the guttering will sit level). Make any adjustments to the position of the knots if necessary.

5. POSITION GUTTERING

Tie the open ends of the rope fixings to two solid points. Slot the guttering through each knotted section, pushing the rope snugly against the end caps. Plant up.

SUITCASE PLANTER

Planters used to be boring — when I was growing up it was considered fancy and ornate if you placed lumps of wood in the ground to raise the height of your flower bed and stained them every few years! Now, however, colour and design is spilling out of our homes and taking over the garden with force. This suitcase planter blends classic style with a gorgeous combination of natural materials, ornately curved reclaimed legs and an injection of colour to complement your plants.

Sourcing a good vintage suitcase isn't too tricky. Charity shops, auctions and antiques dealers usually have a great selection in different materials, colours and styles. Finding one with beautiful old travel labels like the ones you find on old steamer trunks can prove a little harder. Don't despair, however, as there are lots of heritage-style stickers available online. Or you can even add your own stencilled name or initials to give it that period aesthetic and a personal touch.

Not only does this planter look fantastic, but raised planters are easier to maintain — they minimize bending and lifting, making gardening more accessible to those less physically able.

ITEMS TO SOURCE:
- *old leather suitcase*
- *4 wooden furniture legs*
- *OSB (oriented strand board) or plywood sheet*
- *exterior chalk paint*
- *stickers to decorate — optional*
- *plastic sheeting*

1. CLEAN SUITCASE

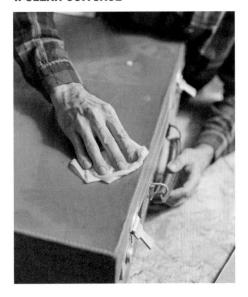

To prepare for painting, clean the case with sugar soap and mask off areas you wish to maintain in their original state, such as buckles, corners and hinges, with tape.

2. FIT BASEBOARD

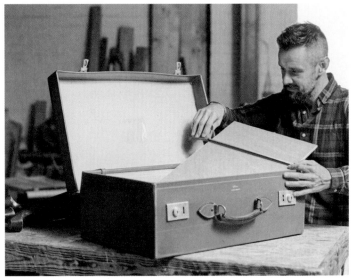

Draw around the base of the suitcase onto the OSB sheet. Using a jigsaw cut out inside this outline by about 1cm (³/₈ inch) smaller than your pencil mark – to ensure a snug fit – and sand to remove sharp edges.

3. PAINT INSIDE AND OUT

Paint the suitcase with exterior chalk paint. Depending on how porous the surface is you may require two coats. When the outside is dry paint the inside, either in the same shade or a complementary colour. If you like, you can apply old-fashioned travel decals to the dry surface.

4. ATTACH LEGS

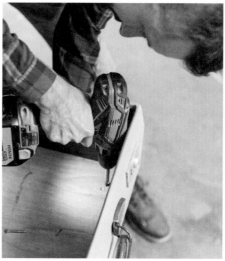

Place the base inside the case then screw through each corner into the top of the legs. Drill drainage holes through the board and the suitcase.

5. LINE CASE AND PLANT

Attach the plastic lining with a staple gun and pierce in a few places to allow water to drain. Fill the lined case with compost or potting soil. Plant up your herbs, the bushier the better!

BOAT FENDER HANGING CONTAINER

Since living on my upcycled houseboat I've been fascinated by many specialist items and bits of kit used on the marina, including fenders. They are found on almost every boat and cost very little, but once they lose their airtight seal they are just thrown in the bin.

This simple upcycle celebrates their beautiful capsule form and creates the perfect portrait-style planter. Cheap to source, easy to transform and practical for years to come — I adore this design.

Fenders come in various designs and shapes so choose wisely. A lot of them have been well used and abused in their life as a boat bumper, but they are often in reasonable condition and can be repurposed as planters. The fact that they are usually made from rubber or plastic makes them durable, easy to work with and available in a variety of colours, although blue or white are most common.

A collection of these at different heights combining several styles would look awesome on land or water — a very cool way of adding a nautical theme to your garden.

ITEMS TO SOURCE:
- *boat fender*
- *rope*

1. CLEAN FENDER

Clean your fender thoroughly with sugar soap, as river water can be full of bacteria that could harm plants.

2. MARK HOLES

Mark the centre of two holes approximately 9cm (3 $\frac{1}{2}$ inches) in diameter, one at the top and one halfway down the fender.

3. DRILL OUT HOLES

Drill out the holes using a hole saw attachment on your drill. You might need a retractable knife (box cutter) to finish cutting out.

4. JOIN HOLES

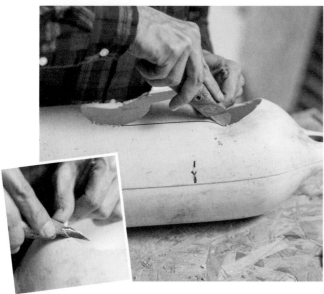

To enlarge the opening, join the two holes with the knife. Smooth the cut edges by dragging the knife blade to get rid of any sharp edges, then sand.

5. DRILL DRAINAGE HOLES

Drill three small drainage holes in the bottom of the fender. Fill the fender with stones first for drainage then compost on top. Tie a piece of nautical rope to the top of the fender and hang. Plant straight into the compost.

TIP: *To clean the edges well, make sure you use a new, sharp blade.*

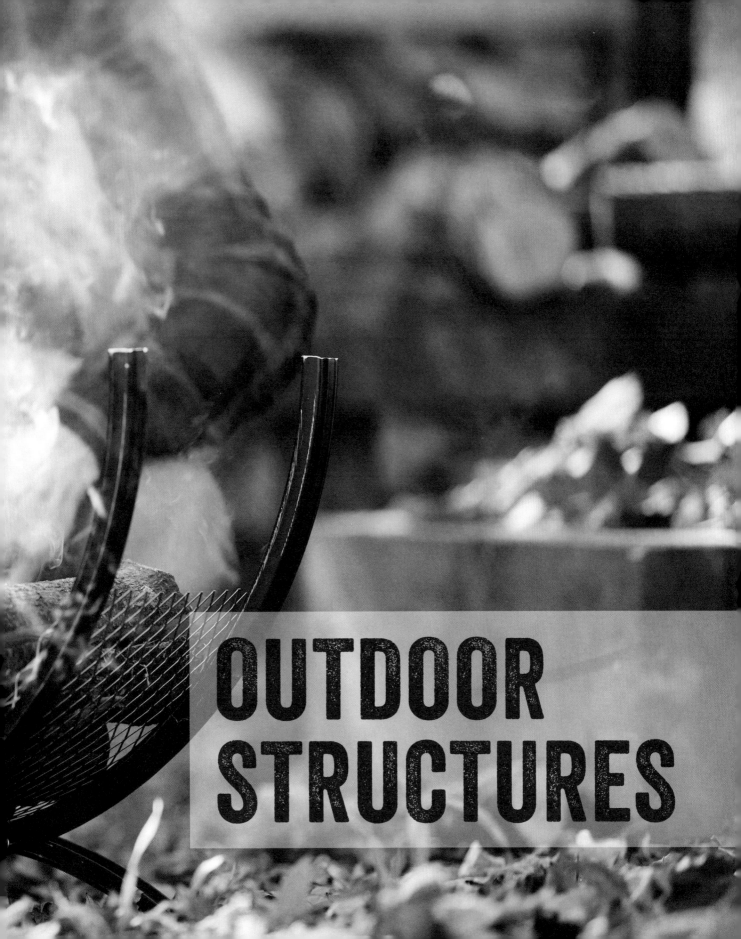

OUTDOOR STRUCTURES

As house prices continue to rise, people like to invest in making the most of their gardens, creating small spaces that can be enjoyed by the entire family. This section doesn't just focus on large items for huge gardens either: there is a self-loading firepit made from an old bike wheel; an upcycled chest of drawers; and even a teepee-inspired play area made from pallets and bed sheets for the kids to enjoy. I've even included a small potting shed, which is ideal when you have limited space, but still need somewhere to do some potting up, sow seeds in trays and store a few hand tools. It is designed to be squeezed into even the smallest of backyards.

This wonderful mix of materials, textures, colours and patterns shows that our homes and gardens can be both practical and playful for partying, while also providing a quiet and tranquil space for relaxing and enjoying downtime with friends and family.

When I started out upcycling my main motivation was to design and make beautiful items that considered our planet. At that time you were either eco-friendly OR you liked good design; the two were rarely combined. Increasingly, however, my work has been more focused on the art of designing and making, both in terms of celebrating forgotten traditional skills as well as utilizing the therapeutic qualities of working with your hands and the mental health benefits associated with any craft activity.

So far so good, well it gets better: upcycling is also a rather good way of saving money! In fact when you think about it upcycling has always existed but with other names, such as make do and mend and being thrifty. I spent my childhood playing on projects in the shed with my dad, making wooden swords, garages for my toy cars and go karts. Upcycling is a great way to spend time with your family while teaching them new skills. Some of the projects in this book take a couple of hours, while others might take a weekend, but either way the chances are you will be saving the planet, saving money, learning new skills and spending quality time with your family - perfect!

PALLET PLAY TENT

Upcycling isn't just for adults — in fact being creative with junk really brings out the child in me! When I was growing up I'm pretty sure I spent my entire school holidays building dens.

The joy of this design is that you can create a magical space in your garden or a den for the kids using just two identical pallets, some fabric or a bed sheet, a hammer and nails. The joy of using pallets the same size is that the wood is already the right length so you don't even need to cut anything! That means you can get the kids involved. What could be better than helping your children create their own teepee out of reclaimed materials and then watching them making it their own, enjoying the great outdoors with their friends.

Of course, if you're a big kid like me you might consider creating a larger, adult-sized teepee using more than two pallets and a couple of bed sheets. To add a real magical sense of fairytale glamour, dress with lots of scatter cushions, some soft throws and a string of battery-operated lights.

ITEMS TO SOURCE:
- *2 pallets of the same size*
- *old bedsheet or large length of fabric*

1. BREAK UP A PALLET

Separate the wood on your pallet using either a pallet breaker or a hammer and breaker bar. Remove the nails by hammering them back through (you may have to straighten them first).

2. MARK A FRAMES

To create a safe, strong structure you will need an A frame at each end. Mark a pallet board width down from the top of the board to create a good overlap.

3. ATTACH END PIECES TO BASE

Set two pieces of pallet together and nail two together to create an A frame for each end. Nail the bottoms to the corners of the pallet base.

SAFETY NOTE: *Make sure that all old nails are removed and any really rough pallet wood is sanded smooth.*

4. ATTACH TOP RAIL

To give additional strength to the structure and to support the fabric cover, nail a cross bar into place where the A frames cross.

5. SECURE COVER

Measure, mark and cut your fabric to size. Throw over the cross bar and secure with nails at the bottom, pulling the fabric taut.

6. MAKE COSY

Dress the interior with cushions and throws. Fairy lights can add glamour.

THREE-DOOR POTTING SHED

Greenhouses and potting sheds are not exactly known for looking beautiful. They are also not normally available to people with a small back garden or with limited access. This three-door shed design utilizes gorgeous old glazed doors, a scaffold board and a bit of corrugated tin to create a usable yet stunning, cute and quirky shelter in which you can prepare and grow herbs and small plants.

Deliberately designed to be built in situ, the construction requires no power cables trailing out of your house, simply a battery-powered drill driver and a hand saw. You can completely strip and repaint the doors first if you wish, especially if your doors are very mismatched in style and finish, but I love the original shabby effect of the paint created by the old paint flaking off.

You can add additional, higher shelving if you require, to suit your needs. The glazing allows light through to your growing plants.

ITEMS TO SOURCE:
- *3 old doors of the same height*
- *hinges (if none on doors)*
- *salvaged scaffold boards for shelves and roof supports*
- *corrugated tin*
- *screws, rubber washers and covers*

1. SCREW DOORS TOGETHER

Clean the doors with sugar soap to remove grime. You can sand and paint them if you desire, but I just love the original patina on these. Fix the three doors together, using the original hinges and screws if present.

2. MARK UP SHELVES

Measure the interior width of the shed, mark and cut out shelves to suit using scaffold boards. (We will use the offcuts to create the wedges for the roof later.) This shelf will be useful for storing plants, potting up and most importantly creating a rigid safe structure.

TAKE YOUR MEASURE FROM THE BACK WALL

3. ATTACH SHELVES

Fit the shelves to the side and rear door to create structural rigidity through the doors using long screws. You can also add battens for extra support. As the shelf may get wet I've decided to wax mine rustic brown.

Tip: As this is a large structure you may need help. Either use clamps or ask a friend.

4. CUT ROOF SUPPORTS

Mark and cut the wedges to sit on top of the side doors. Angle from higher at the front to lower at the back – this will create a natural run-off for water, sloping away from the door to prevent drips as you enter.

5. PAINT AND FIX WEDGES

Paint or wax the wedges and front support. I've gone for a matching subtle colour, but you could create a feature using a bold colour if you're feeling brave.

6. CUT FRONT PIECE

Using another offcut of scaffold board create a support for the roof across the front of the shed.

7. CUT TIN FOR ROOF

Measure your structure and add about 5cm (2 inches) on each edge to make sure you have an overhang large enough to prevent driving rain, but not so big that the wind gets in underneath. Cut and sand the rough edges carefully using an angle grinder.

8. ATTACH ROOF

Fit the corrugated tin roof using screws with rubber washers and covers. Fit these on the higher corrugations to prevent water sitting in the troughs seeping through the holes.
You can also add a few hooks to hang tools from, if you like. Fill with plants and admire your handy work. This design is fantastic when space is limited in city dwellings and apartments – it could even be installed on a balcony and requires very little access.

BICYCLE WHEEL FIREPIT

The great outdoors is something that has been very close to my heart since I was a small child. I was a cub scout, and every year we went caravanning as a family. To maximize the time you can spend outside in the colder months, and even to extend chillier summer evenings, a fire is essential. What I love about this design is that it is lightweight and therefore extremely portable; it repurposes something that has already travelled around outdoors; and it also combines beautiful aesthetics with clever engineering - my perfect combination!

It can be very frustrating when you get distracted or leave a fire and it goes out. This design allows you to preload the pit with round logs that simply roll into the centre as the previous log burns away, removing the need for you to keep loading the fire.

Produced with only threaded bars and some mesh, this design is lightweight, simple and satisfying to make and reuses a pair of old dented bicycle wheels that would otherwise be thrown away.

ITEMS TO SOURCE:
- *2 old bicycle wheels*
- *threaded bars, washers and nuts*
- *wire mesh*

1. REMOVE TYRES

Using a flat-head screwdriver or a chisel, work around the tyre, loosening it until the metal wheel structure will pop free. Repeat for the other tyre.

2. REMOVE SPOKES

Use the first wheel for the base supports — you are going to remove one third of the wheel for each one. Mark your wheel on the rim then remove using a slitting disc on a grinder or hacksaw. Cut the rim into sections.

3. CUT SECOND WHEEL IN HALF

Remove the spokes from the second wheel and then cut the wheel in half. These will form the main section of the fire base.

4. NEATEN ENDS

Sand the sharp edges smooth with a metal file.

5. LINE UP BASE

Position your smaller bases against the semicircular pieces, as shown in the sketch, and mark up.

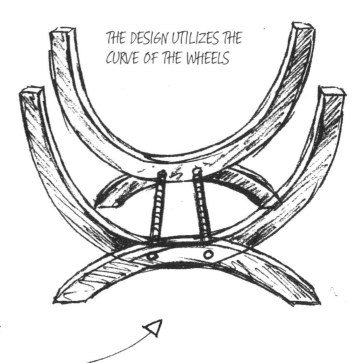

THE DESIGN UTILIZES THE CURVE OF THE WHEELS

6. DRILL THROUGH RIMS

Drill holes in the wheel rims on the marks, then de-burr using a larger drill or countersunk bit.

7. CUT THREADED ROD

Cut the threaded rod to the right length using a junior hacksaw. File the ends smooth.

8. BOLT TOGETHER

Bolt through the wheels to form the two halves and join them together using washers and nuts.

9. ATTACH MESH BASE

TIP: *You can spray the entire construction with heat-resistant stove paint if required.*

Cut the wire mesh to size using wire cutters. It doesn't need to extend all the way up the wheel rims as the stacked logs will stay in place. Wrap the edges of the mesh neatly around the wheel rims to secure it in place.

10. LOAD LOGS

Fill the pit with round logs cut neatly to fit, then sit back in wonder as the fire self-fills as it burns!

DRESSING TABLE PLANT DISPLAY

There is something quite magical about seeing ornate interior furniture out of context in an outdoor environment. Chests of drawers such as this dressing table can be purchased for very little, particularly if they have some surface damage. That doesn't matter, of course, as I chose to paint the drawers with exterior chalk paint.

I have been quite bold with my decoration for this piece. Not only have I used bright complementary colours, but I've also applied a crackle glaze between the two coats of paint to add a vintage, distressed look, which I think works perfectly with the style of this piece. The mirror is a nice bonus. It adds a splash of opulence while also creating the illusion of more space and light.

I filled the drawers with potted plants so I can change the display through the seasons. You could line the drawers with heavy plastic and drill some drainage holes if you want to plant directly into them, but the weight of the soil will make them very heavy to handle.

ITEMS TO SOURCE:
- *a retro dressing table with deep drawers, ideally made from solid timber to withstand weather*
- *exterior chalk paint*
- *crackle glaze*

1. PREPARE WOODWORK

Source a retro dressing table with drawers. Remove the drawers and clean the entire thing with sugar soap. Even though we are going to use chalk paint, which requires less surface preparation, you still need a good clean surface.

2. PAINT THE CARCASS

Chalk paint the exterior carcass. I have chosen a rather striking yet garden-friendly pea-soup green.

3. REMOVE DRAWER FURNITURE

Remove the drawer handles and keep them safe — I always screw the bolts back in the handles so I don't lose them. Paint the drawers in the same colour as the carcass (this sounds a bit boring but don't worry, I promise it won't be!).

4. APPLY CRACKLE GLAZE

Once the base coat on the drawers has dried it's time to apply a coat of clear crackle glaze. Apply the crackle glaze with a brush in the same direction as the first coat of paint and allow to dry.

Apply a very generous second coat of paint in a contrasting colour (I've chosen plum pudding) at right angles to the crackle. As the paint begins to dry you can see the crackle coming through. (Do NOT go over the paint again – I've done this before and it can go horribly wrong!)

5. REATTACH HANDLES

Once all paint is dry, fit handles then remount the mirror. If you do want to line the drawers with plastic, this is the time to do it. And don't forget to add some drainage holes in the base of each drawer.

6. FILL WITH PLANTS

Reassemble the drawers with the bottom one furthest out. Fill the drawers with a variety of potted plants, choosing some with foliage that spills over the edges.

EATING + ENTERTAINING

In the warm summer months there is no better way to entertain your guests than in the garden. Watching the sun set with friends while enjoying good food and drink is one of my favourite pastimes.

Not only is entertaining outdoors more fun, but it can also save you heaps of money. Making items from scrap can cost little more than your time, and your results become the talking point of your dinner party. Whether it's saving an old item of garden furniture but giving it a contemporary twist; rescuing something out of a skip (dumpster); or repurposing an item from the house, one thing is for sure: it's always better to upcycle this stuff for use in your garden than send it to landfill.

Of course, these items don't have to be restricted to your own backyard. Designs like the bicycle picnic set are an ingenious way of taking your upcycled creations on any adventure. With the simple addition of a leather belt even the toolbox barbecue can easily be transported to your favourite woodland retreat to enjoy with your mates.

The barbecue toolbox is also a prime example of the way upcycling can allow you to celebrate the emotional element of design. The knowledge that this gorgeous portable barbecue was actually my first-ever toolbox only makes the act of entertaining even more fun, and sharing it with friends allows those memories to live on. This emotional attachment is unique to repurposed items: that feeling can never be replicated when buying new products, however excited we are about our purchases.

When it comes to imagination, we all know that children win hands down, and half of the enjoyment is actually *making* games, not just playing them. In this digital age, when most entertainment involves gadgets, gizmos and bright flashing lights, it's wonderful to witness children and adults alike laughing and having fun with nothing but some old lumps of wood, a ball of string and some old tin cans.

Creating toys and games from reclaimed materials means they look great, help the planet and stand the test of time, while creating memories to last a lifetime.

TOOLBOX BARBECUE

If there are three things that make me happy in life, they are upcycling, tools and eating good food with friends. I've had this particular toolbox in my workshop since I started my business — I purchased it with the money I received from my first sale. It's a bit battered and has seen better days, but I couldn't part with it for sentimental reasons. Then, while drinking tea and stroking my beard, searching for inspiration, I had a moment of madness: what if I could upcycle it into the ultimate portable barbecue?

I always strive to combine form and function, so I was keen to have a series of cooking levels that could be varied for searing, cooking and keeping food warm. The toolbox is made from the same thickness of metal as most barbecues, and with several drawers of varying depths it seemed perfect for what I needed it to do. The top compartment offered an obvious cache for storing tongs, skewers and other essential cooking tools. It just needed the addition of carry handles, so you can take your new upcycled, self-contained barbecue wherever you fancy, whether it's the back garden, a festival or the nearest beach. I knew I wanted to produce a barbecue for this book that was unique and quirky, and here was the answer.

ITEMS TO SOURCE:
- *metal toolbox with drawers*
- *old barbecue grills*
- *old leather belt*
- *metal rivets*

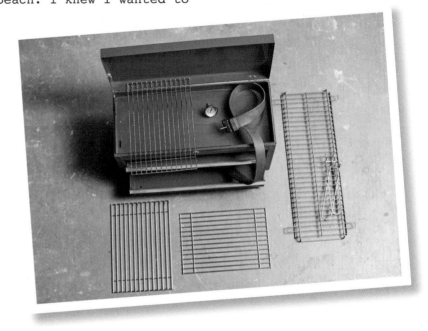

1. MARK OUT DRAWERS

Empty your tools from the toolbox, give them a clean and a new home! Mark out the bottoms of the drawers to be cut, keeping a lipped frame all round to locate the grill. When cutting out a square or rectangle the corners can be tricky and create weak points. If you drill a hole in each corner before you cut, it makes for a neater, stronger result.

TIP: Cone cutters are a great versatile tool to have around your workshop. They allow you to drill a variety of hole sizes the further up the cone you go, ideal for cutting these corner holes in this steel.

2. CUT OUT BASES

Using an angle grinder with a cutting disc, remove the bases of the drawers. Watch out for flying sparks – wear appropriate clothing and safety goggles or a welder's mask to protect your eyes.

3. SMOOTH EDGES

Sand the cut edges with a sanding disc on your grinder. (Remember to disconnect the power when changing attachments!) To finish, use a small round file to get right into the corners.

4. CUT GRILLS TO SIZE

Using the natural dimensions of the salvaged barbecue grills, decide which way round they are going to be used, maintaining as much structural integrity as possible. Trim to fit with your grinder then sand the cut edges to ensure they are not sharp.

5. ASSEMBLE

I even managed to rescue the temperature gauge from the donor barbecue, so simply drilled a hole and bolted it on! Now assemble the barbecue by dropping in the grills.

6. ATTACH STRAP

To increase portability I added a brown leather strap made from an old belt. Cut the belt to length then drill holes through (or use the existing belt holes) and rivet the belt in place, using the original carry handles on the toolbox as your attachment point.

TIN CAN GAME

Some of my fondest memories growing up are of times spent in my garden making toys and games out of old branches and twigs. My poor mum was never able to use the washing up liquid (dish soap) from the plastic bottle — as soon as it arrived from the shops I would empty the contents into a mug so I could turn the bottle into a rocket, the body of an animal or a ball thrower! With a vivid imagination, children will happily play like this for hours, benefitting from lots of fresh air and improving hand-eye coordination. This simple tin can game provides creative children with hours of fun, and can be constantly adapted and updated to make it suitable for children of all ages and abilities.

I love how raw this upcycle looks, from the exposed corrugations on the tin cans to the rustic rope. Source a variety of tin cans. You can either use the standard-sized tins from home, or ask at a local café if they can give you some bigger tins. This project takes less than an hour to produce an item that will provide hours of fun for the entire family. I suspect once the kids have gone the adults will get just as much fun playing.

ITEMS TO SOURCE:
- *a selection of old tin cans of different sizes*
- *exterior chalk paint*
- *rope — thick and thin*

1. SET UP ROPE

Clean your cans thoroughly and remove all the labels. Paint some in different colours, and retain some in the original metal finish for variety. Make sure they don't have any sharp edges – you can tidy these with a file if required. Suspend a length of rope from some tree trunks or any other suitable mounting points.

2. HANG LOOPS

Tie thinner pieces of rope in loops in which the cans will sit. I created two loops of the same size with a knot where they meet.

3. SUSPEND CANS

Sit your can in the rope frame and secure at the top by tying another piece of rope around the top edge. Cut off any excess rope. A couple of loose stones can be used to weight the can so it sits snugly.

4. ARRANGE CANS

Hang your cans at random heights to create a more challenging game. This arrangement combined with the random colours and sizes creates something that is fun to play but also looks great!

5. MAKE ROPE BALLS

Now you could just use tennis balls for this game, but I think it's even more fun to make the balls from left-over rope! Start by wrapping the string around your finger, trapping in the loose end as you go. Once you have created the ball, simply tuck in the cut end. Now have a go!

BICYCLE PICNIC SET

In the past few years cycling has become hugely popular, with serious cyclists embracing high-tech mountain bikes, a love of Lycra and imbibing health snacks. The problem is that I love to cycle, but I'd rather ride my old road bike, wear my normal clothes and take a picnic to a gorgeous outdoor location than grab a protein bar en route! This project indulges all of those elements, and incorporates some of my favourite materials — wood, fabric and glass. It even uses one of my favourite tools - the sliding bevel. While it is perfectly possible to carry your food and drink in a backpack, that doesn't give you a table to rest your drinks and nibbles on when you get to your location.

This design is really good fun to make, can be produced in your garage at home, and once complete it will be the envy of all other cyclists and picnic goers. The picnic box does add weight to your bicycle, but that might be a very useful way of burning off all that cheese and wine!

ITEMS TO SOURCE:
- *a usable bicycle*
- *a sheet of plywood*
- *chalkboard paint*
- *wax*
- *salvaged pallet wood*
- *3 old leather belts*
- *metal rivets*
- *jam jar lids*
- *piece of fabric*
- *metal butt hinges*

1. TAKE MEASUREMENTS

To create the box shape, measure your bike frame, including the different angles, using a sliding bevel or tape measure.

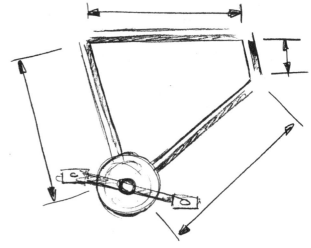

MAKE A NOTE OF THE KEY DIMENSIONS

2. CUT BOX SHAPES

Draw the shape you've just measured – which will be for your front door and back section – onto plywood. Cut out two pieces using a hand saw then sand the edges.

3. PAINT AND FINISH

Paint the front and the back pieces with chalkboard paint, then to make the whole thing watertight char the side edges (see page 86 for how to do this), then wax them.

4. CUT SIDE AND INTERNAL PIECES

Measure, mark and cut out each length from pallet wood, angling cut ends as necessary to fit. Sand the rough edges.

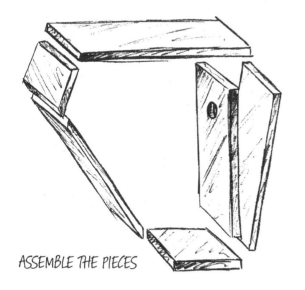

ASSEMBLE THE PIECES

5. MAKE BOTTLE HOLDER

Drill a hole in the centre upright just bigger than the neck of a bottle.

6. MAKE OUTER FRAME

Assemble the components together, using a hammer and nails. Lay the whole structure flat on the floor or a bench to make sure it's flush. Then nail the frame to the back piece.

7. ADD STRAPS

Fit the leather tabs – taken from the strap ends of old leather belts – for fixing the box to the bike frame. Attach with metal rivets.

8. FIX JAR LIDS

Screw jam jar lids to the upright insert in the box, then screw the jam jar on, creating a portable drinking glass!

9. LINE AND ATTACH DOOR

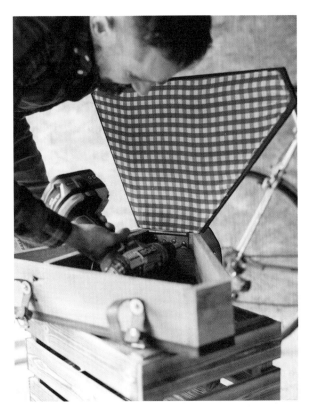

Apply the fabric to the inside face of the front piece, or door, using a staple gun. Screw the door to the box using small metal butt hinges.

10. CUT LONG STRAP

Cut another leather belt to length, recreating a nicely curved end.

11. ATTACH HANDLE

Fix the strap in two places to the back of the picnic box using metal rivets and a rivet gun.

12. FIT TO BICYCLE

Slot the box in the bicycle frame and attach to the cross bar with the two small straps. Pull up and tighten the long strap to close the box, and release it when you have arrived at your chosen destination to suspend your picnic table!

GIANT DOMINO SET

In a time when tablets, PlayStation and mobile (cell) phones didn't exist we used to play simple games like Scrabble, chess and dominoes. By making these games out of durable materials you can share these experiences with your children and friends while entertaining them outdoors. Giant games are always great fun at any party, and these dominoes also look pretty cool, with their charred finish. The charring technique makes it easy to see the number dots, brings out the gorgeous grain of the scaffold board and also makes the wood water-repellent.

It is possible to paint the dots onto the wood, but in outdoor conditions where they will be exposed to the elements I think drilling the circular holes will last a lot longer and means they can be thrown around and stored in their beautiful apple crate box without concern for the paint scratching off.

ITEMS TO SOURCE:
• old scaffold boards — building sites or scaffold companies usually have lots of small offcuts lying around, which are ideal
• old wooden fruit crates for storage

1. CUT DOMINO PIECES

Cut the scaffold boards to equal-sized lengths with a hand saw. Each piece should be 40cm (16 inches) long, and you will need at least 28 pieces in total.

2. SAND

Sand the pieces all over till they are completely smooth. An electric mouse sander will make quick work of this.

3. CHAR SURFACE

Char each domino piece all over, including the side edges, with a gas blow torch to darken the wood colour, bring out the grain and make the dominoes waterproof.

TIP: A standard, or 'double-six' domino set uses 28 pieces. For the arrangement of the dots, including blanks and double tiles, you can find clear diagrams online.

4. MARK HALFWAY LINE

Measure and mark the halfway point on each piece. Saw a shallow groove with a hand saw. Mark up and dot the centres of the number holes with a pencil.

5. DRILL NUMBER HOLES

Using a Forstner drill bit, drill 4cm (1$\frac{1}{2}$ inch) diameter dots about 1cm ($\frac{3}{8}$ inch) deep. Wax the entire board with clear furniture wax.

Find a smooth stretch of lawn and play!

FURNITURE

It's fair to say that for many years outdoor furniture was restricted to deckchairs and uncomfortable wooden patio sets. In this chapter you will find a selection of designs showing how you can take tired old interior furniture and reinvent it to be enjoyed in the garden.

Ever planted up an old dining chair or covered a cheap flatpack coffee table in concrete? Me neither, but it was great fun experimenting and I hope you'll agree the results look awesome! Experimenting with these new materials not only creates a wonderful-looking piece of outdoor furniture, but also increases their durability to ensure they are enjoyed for years to come.

Throw into the mix a simple way to upcycle a tired old picnic bench along with a design to find a use for all those old single dining chairs you can pick up secondhand. I thoroughly enjoyed the creations you see here in the furniture chapter — after all, upcycling furniture is where it all started for me.

When you mention upcycling to most people they immediately think of painting old furniture. I love this process and recently I have seen some outstanding pieces - not just painted all one block colour but combining finishes such as wallpaper, ombre effects, decoupage, adding bespoke handles, using complementary colours or leaving certain areas natural timber. These all result in a much more considered and well-designed look in my opinion.

Repurposing existing items and giving them a new lease of life isn't the only way to upcycle. I really enjoy designing, inventing and engineering new products created from reclaimed materials. In our workshop we spend a lot of time breaking up old pallets, sanding back floorboards and trimming broken bits from scaffold boards. Reclaimed metal is one of my favourite materials to scavenge at the moment: copper, zinc-plated tin and even rusty steel are all wonderful materials to use for new designs. Part of the joy of using these old materials is the fact that they blend in a lot more subtly in a garden setting when they are naturally worn, rather than introducing a bright and shiny brand-new item.

PICNIC BENCH DRINKS COOLER

How many tired old picnic benches do you see just sitting there feeling sorry for themselves? Usually they are in pretty good condition structurally — they just need a bit of a makeover. You could just sand one back and apply some oil or a lick of paint, but why not add a bit of practical yet fun functionality with the addition of a galvanized plant trough to hold iced drinks or even candles?

This is a relatively simple upcycle that requires very few tools and even reuses the existing nails and offcuts of wood. What makes this project even easier is that it only requires hand tools, so you can work on the bench outside in situ, rather than trying to dismantle and get it inside.

These old wooden picnic benches can be picked up very cheaply or sometimes even for free. They are typically not very exciting, but with this simple addition it's possible to convert a sad-looking old bench into a centrepiece for your parties.

ITEMS TO SOURCE:
* *old picnic bench*
* *galvanized metal plant trough*

1. REMOVE CENTRE PLANKS

Carefully remove the three central boards from the bench. Sometimes these are attached using screws. If they have used nails you may need to use a hammer. Knock through any old nails from the underside so you can reuse them.

TIP: When knocking wooden items apart use a scrap piece of wood to hit against to prevent damaging the good surface.

2. MEASURE

Place your metal container in the gap, pushing the boards either side up to it to support it under the rim. Find and mark the centre using a tape measure and mark it. Hammer the boards either side into their new positions.

3. SECURE TROUGH

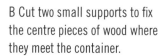
A Knock the nails back in to resecure the two boards either side of the trough.

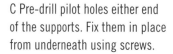
B Cut two small supports to fix the centre pieces of wood where they meet the container.

C Pre-drill pilot holes either end of the supports. Fix them in place from underneath using screws.

D Place the centre top pieces of wood in location then mark, trim to length and nail into place.

4. FILL WITH ICE

You can now load up your metal trough with ice and keep your drinks bottles cool when you entertain. The trough will lift out easily so you can pour out the melted ice.

CHAIR SWING

As we grow up there are some activities we loved to do as children that society tells us we shouldn't indulge in any more as adults - swinging is one of those pastimes. What better item to use to create a swing that is as comfortable for adults to use as for children than an old wooden pub chair? Pub chairs, usually an unappealing dark brown and smelling a bit of stale beer, look a bit sad. But they are structurally sound, have gorgeous curves and are ergonomically perfect. This project celebrates these qualities and adds a contemporary twist in terms of both style and purpose — this swing functions as well as it looks!

By attaching rustic rope and chopping the legs, you can turn a once unloved chair into a fun and enjoyable piece of garden furniture for years to come. Kids will suddenly realize that you can have a lot of fun without the need for technology and touch screens!

ITEMS TO SOURCE:
- *old wooden chair*
- *strong, thick rope*
- *exterior chalk paint*
- *Danish oil*

1. MARK OUT CUTS

Mark cutting lines on all four legs and the back rest. Draw around something circular — I used some handy masking tape — to get two matching curves.

2. TRIM LEGS

Reduce the length of the legs using a hand saw, then sand the bases smooth.

TIP: Use your thumb as a steady rest for the saw blade.

3. REDUCE BACK REST

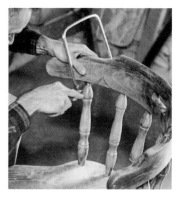

Saw away the two outer back spindles using a Japanese saw, hand saw or an electric saw.

Trim the back rest following the marked lines using a coping saw, then sand smooth.

4. ADD ROPE AND SAND

Measure and drill four holes for the rope, making sure they are balanced on either side. If possible drill through the holes left by the spindles. Sand all over, then brush off the dust. Paint the legs and spindles with outdoor chalk paint. Apply Danish oil to the seat base and back rest to nourish and protect the wood. Tie rope through the holes and onto a branch using a good secure knot.

5. HANG

CONCRETE-COVERED TABLE

Cheap flatpack chipboard furniture is often criticized in the upcycling community. It can contribute to the huge landfill problem, as it's not easy to upcycle such items: you cannot always get a good fixing into these lightweight items, as you more easily can with solid timber furniture. Chipboard is not waterproof, and so not suitable to be left outdoors.

But it does have its benefits. It's affordable, so people with less disposable cash can buy into good-looking design; it is lightweight and flatpack, so better for the planet in terms of shipping; and some of it is actually quite stylish. This simple table lends itself perfectly to a makeover, due to its slab-sided design and size. By skimming the entire exterior surface with a mix of concrete and PVA glue, you can create a table that looks sleek and contemporary and that's weatherproof for use outdoors — it should last for years. The equivalent table produced from solid concrete would be heavy, expensive and a lot less fun to produce!

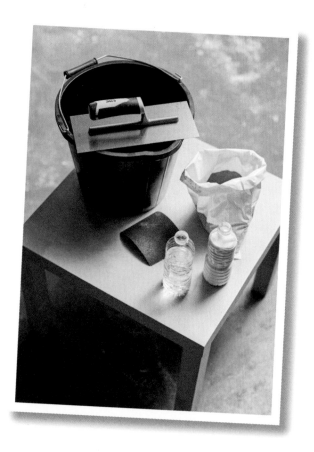

ITEMS TO SOURCE:
- *Flatpack table — this one is from IKEA*
- *concrete and sand dry mix*
- *PVA glue*
- *lacquer or varnish to finish*

1. PREPARE SURFACE

Source an appropriate cheap flatpack chipboard coffee table. It can be scratched, but avoid using one that is structurally damaged. Sand lightly all over to create a key on the surface (120 grit sandpaper should be good for this). Clean the table all over using sugar soap and a soft cloth.

2. COAT WITH PVA

Paint the table with a coat of undiluted PVA glue. This will help the cement coating to stick, and will also help the table to stay watertight – essential for outdoor use.

3. MAKE UP CEMENT

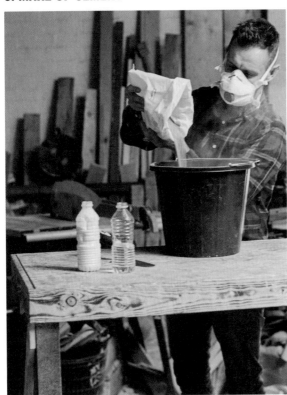

I used a concrete mix that is three parts sand to one part cement, but instead of adding the recommended amount of water I used half water, half PVA glue, with a squirt of washing up liquid (dish soap). Mix thoroughly so you have a smooth consistency with no lumps.

4. SKIM

Apply a first coat all over the top and outside of the table with a trowel. Once dry, turn over and coat the underside in exactly the same way. Each coat should be about 2mm (1/8 inch) thick.

5. APPLY FINAL COAT

Finally apply a second coat all over the top, which is where the table will receive the most wear and tear. I personally like to see the trowel marks, but feel free to sand smooth if you require a more contemporary polished effect. Apply a few coats of varnish or lacquer, making sure it doesn't react with the concrete by testing a small, hidden area first.

LIVING CHAIR

The chair used for this project has been kicking around my workshop for years, and I've always wanted to create something special with it. The gorgeous contours and wood tones really lend themselves to upcycling such a chair into a wonderful and opulent feature piece to sit proudly at the head of any al fresco dining event.

Cutting into the fabric was a very weird and scary experience that doesn't come naturally to a lover of furniture, but the results are simply stunning. Any upholstered chair could be used for this project to create a real fairytale throne of a chair that remains usable if you are careful about how you position the planting pockets. Ivy is the perfect plant to use as it will establish quickly, it doesn't require a huge amount of soil and will tolerate some neglect and even dry conditions. For a bit of colour you could use a miniature or patio rose, but this is probably best planted in the seat rather than the back of the chair, and you will need to add some plant food to the soil to keep it in good condition. For a quick splash of colour you can do as I have and simply push some cut flowers into the holes.

ITEMS TO SOURCE:
- *old upholstered upright chair*
- *upholstery paint*
- *wood wax*

1. PAINT

Sand and clean the chair and paint the upholstery. We used green to blend into the environment, but you could choose a bolder colour to make a statement piece.

2. WAX

Wax the exposed wood to make it waterproof — we used a dark brown shade.

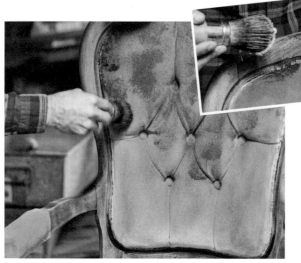

TIP: Don't panic if you get wax on the fabric. You can cover this up by delicately waxing the rest of the fabric to give an aged look.

3. PLANT UP

In suitable areas such as the corners of the back rest and the seat cushion, cut horizontal slots to create planting pockets. Remove some of the padding and fill these pockets with potting soil appropriate for the type of plants you wish to plant. Insert climbing plants such as ivy, which will flow beautifully over the contours of the chair. Water well to get them established. For a temporary display you can add some flowering plants in complementary colours to really create impact. When you are ready, set the chair in position in your garden.

LIGHTING + ACCESSORIES

've said for years that the addition of good lighting and accessories can completely transform a design. This is definitely the case when it comes to upcycling outdoors.

Often dinner parties and barbecues can run into the evening, and as the sun falls there is no better way to inject a bit of wow factor than the glow of some good ambient lighting. Candles and garden flares have always been popular, but there is a lot more choice now, with new technology offering a variety of options, from festoon lights to LED strings. You need practical items of furniture, but when it comes to creating an instant and affordable impact it's all about the finishing touches, and adding a bit of humour and individuality in the garden.

Interior design rules can also be applied outdoors. Concepts such as displaying items in odd numbers - typically three works well — contrasting and complementary colours are important, as is mixing materials and textures.

It's one thing creating a beautiful piece of upcycled furniture but it's so important to complete the design with the right accessories. So often I attend craft fairs and makers' markets where the artisan has made something wonderful, but completely neglected to show potential buyers how the design may look in their own home. By adding a few plants, candles, ornaments and picture frames you can really bring your piece to life. This is also essential for successful product photography. People are far more likely to buy an item that thay can visualize in their own homes, so help them out with this process.

If you are considering becoming a professional upcycler it's important to pitch your products to the right customer at the correct price and appropriate size. A lot of designers are drawn to producing large items with expensive price tags. However, if you design smaller accessories which can be taken home easily and which sell at a lower price point, such as the ones in this chapter, you may find more success. Smaller designs are also usually cheaper to produce, more compact to store and transport, easier to ship and a simpler purchase for your customers, who may have limited space.

BIRD CAGE LIGHTS

In the interior design world all things caged wire have become popular, but nothing is quite so popular as the wonderful form of a bird cage — there is something ever so beautiful about the curved silhouette. Once cleaned up these cages are stunning, and the addition of some sparkly lights creates something truly magical. I do sometimes get concerned about modifying vintage and collectible items with inherent value, so this design allows you to create a gorgeous centrepiece lamp without having to actually destroy or alter the original elegant bird cage.

We have used battery-powered fairy lights for ease, but you could also use some solar-powered ones, if you are careful about where you site the charging sensors, and depending on the tree coverage. For a more permanent arrangement you could even hard wire some lights into your house if you have the skills or can call on the services of a qualified electrician.

ITEMS TO SOURCE:
* *old metal bird cage, the more decorative the better*
* *metal spray paint*
* *string of lights*
* *old metal chain*
* *butcher's hook*

1. CLEAN CAGE

Remove any bits of the bird cage that you don't want, such as plastic food and water bowls. Slide out the base. Clean the cage carefully with sugar soap. If you are at all susceptible, wear a dust mask and gloves, as bird droppings are not good for your respiratory system.

2. PAINT BATTERY PACK

If you don't like the existing finish and colour of your cage, you could spray paint it. I was happy with the worn and mottled metallic finish so left this one in its original state. But I wanted to disguise the black plastic battery pack, so it doesn't show inside the cage, so I sprayed it to match.

3. ARRANGE LIGHTS

Thread the lights around the bars of the cage, pushing some bulbs out through the bars. Replace the base, placing the battery pack in one corner.

Finally, attach a metal chain using a butcher's hook so you can hang the cage from a tree.

TIP: *By having the lights on when threading it allows you to see the distribution of light.*

4. ADD CHAIN

FESTOON LAMPSHADES

Lighting is a very simple and clever way of creating a lovely warm ambiance for any outdoor event. Festoon lighting is currently very popular, with different designs and coloured bulbs available. Most are LED and connect to your home electricity supply, but some come with battery packs, and you can even buy solar-powered ones, which are great if you want to light up an area at the bottom of your garden, at a distance from your house. But though useful, I think festoon lights lack a bit of upcycled personality!

Old lampshades can be found in charity shops and thrift stores for very little money, in a variety of styles and conditions. The better-looking shades can be cleaned up and used as they are, if the fabric is physically fine. If they are lacking in the style stakes you can paint them. And even those that are completely ruined and perhaps ripped have a place; you can strip them completely and make a feature of the frame itself. I think the more random the selection the better: mix and match styles and celebrate the vintage and kitsch designs of old.

Incorporating a couple of the hottest current trends in lighting design — exposed lightbulbs and festoon lighting — this imaginative arrangement quickly transforms any garden into a beautiful entertainment space.

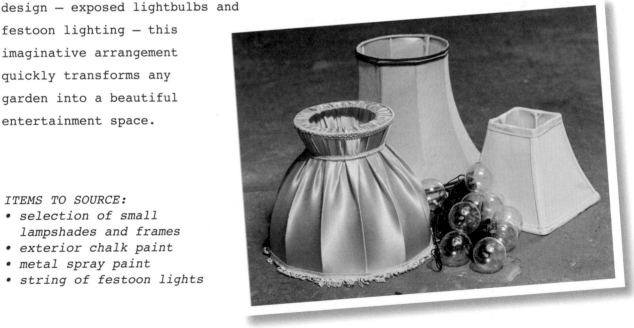

ITEMS TO SOURCE:
- *selection of small lampshades and frames*
- *exterior chalk paint*
- *metal spray paint*
- *string of festoon lights*

1. SOURCE

Visit your local charity shop, car boot sale or yard sale, and source ten random old lampshades, the brighter and more eclectic the better! Go for lots of different shapes and styles, from ruched and fringed to bold and contemporary. Frame shapes can vary from basic drums to rounded, flared and square. The condition is not so important, as you can upgrade them, but check that the mounting ring is intact so you can attach the festoon bulb.

2. PREPARE

If the shades are in good condition just give them a clean with a damp cloth. If the shades are a bit dull or dirty give them a coat of colourful exterior chalk paint, either in one solid block colour, or each panel a different shade. If the cover is damaged then simply strip off the fabric and spray paint the frame.

3. FIT LIGHTS

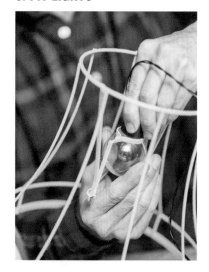

Adapt the mounting ring to suit the festoon light string if required, by squeezing with pliers. Fit the lampshades to the festoon bulbs then simply hang and wait for dusk to appreciate the display.

BIRD BOX FORK MAN

Design, and specifically upcycled design, should in my opinion be fun and playful, and this bird box fork man is certainly both of those things!

Not everyone has a large garden with room for sheds and large amounts of storage. This cute little garden character provides storage space for garden tools, a display area and even incorporates a bird box into the design to encourage wildlife into your garden. If you don't have trees in your back garden, but wish to put up a bird box, you may wish to try this simple idea. One of the best aspects about this design is that it doesn't mean you lose out on being able to use the tools for their original purpose; the clever use of spring clips means that they are removable and are simply stored and ready for action.

I have used the forks and trowel that my parents used when I was growing up, so this piece has added sentimentality for me - I am a firm believer that good design should provoke emotion.

ITEMS TO SOURCE:
- *wooden crate*
- *spring clips*
- *large garden fork*
- *bird box*
- *assorted garden hand tools*
- *wax*

1. MEASURE AND MARK

Line up the handle of the large fork on the crate base. Mark the position of the clip.

2. SCREW

Screw the first spring clip in place as marked.

3. POSITION TOP CLIPS

Use two spring clips on the top vertical section of the handle for balance. Place the fork in position, making sure it is firmly held in place by the first clip, then mark the position for the top clips. Screw these in place.

4. ADD SIDE CLIPS

To form the 'arms' for your man, measure and fix the clips on either side for the hand tools.

5. ATTACH BIRD BOX

For the 'head', attach the bird box to the apple crate 'body', screwing from underneath. This way it can be easily removed if you want to move it around.

6. ASSEMBLE

Sand and wax all wooden components. Clip the crate body to the large fork and drive firmly into the ground. Add the bird box. Finally clip the hand tools in place for the arms.

DOG FEEDING STATION

Now I love my puppy Luna, I really do. But that doesn't mean I've spent hours designing my home interior and outside space, only to place a generic bone-printed dog bowl on the floor. This is not in keeping with the rest of the design theme, and would jar for me every time I saw it. On a practical level, feeding at floor level is not ideal for larger dogs, who should eat and drink from a higher position to prevent bloating.

To tackle this canine conundrum, the answer for me was to create this very simple slot-together design, which allows you to support your own choice of household ceramic bowls to hold food and water, with a decoration that complements the overall design ethos of the space. You could even choose bowls that match your own crockery.

The slot-together design is not only very pleasing on the eye, it makes it easy to produce. It can be quickly taken apart for cleaning or taking away with you on dog walks, holidays, visits to friends or to work. It can be packed flat, so is compact for transporting in the car.

ITEMS TO SOURCE:
- *ceramic bowls*
- *old scaffold boards or similar thick wood*
- *wax*

1. MEASURE AND TRACE

Draw around your chosen bowl to get your key dimensions. Fill in other curves freehand, setting an overall height suitable for your dog. Add a centre line, so that your design will be perfectly symmetrical. You will need to create three intersecting pieces, as shown opposite. Transfer the templates to the wood, flipping over the template to mark both sides.

2. CUT OUT

Cut out all external lines and the indentations for the bowls to sit in using a jigsaw.

3. DRILL HOLES FOR SLOTS

To prevent the wood splitting, drill a hole in the centre where the boards are to intersect, using a hole saw.

4. MARK OUT CUTS

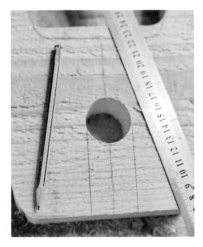

Mark lines for cuts, either side of the hole, to form the slots.

TIP: When drilling the hole have a spare piece of wood clamped securely underneath so you can go all the way through.

5. CUT AND CHECK SLOTS

Using a jigsaw, cut along the marked lines either side of the hole to form your slots. Make the other slots the same way, then check they fit. Sand if necessary to allow a smooth fit.

6. FINISH

Sand and wax all of the surfaces to remove sharp edges and make waterproof. You could paint the wood a bright colour using exterior chalk paint, but I prefer a natural finish that really highlights the wood grain.

Slot the pieces together and insert the bowls. Load up with food and water and your dog is good to go!

7. ASSEMBLE

TOOLS +
TECHNIQUES

OUTDOOR TOOLBOX

When you are upcycling outdoors it is likely you will need to use a few power tools. While they can be an upfront cost for your project, if you buy wisely and look after them they will last a long time and enable you to produce many other creations. Tools for the keen amateur are becoming increasingly affordable. If you are starting from scratch I predict you could set yourself up with the basic hand tools, including a toolbox, for £100 ($130). Then you can add a few power tools for around an additional £200 ($260).

I like to treat myself with every job I do. I consider it an investment when adding to my collection - upcycling projects become easier, quicker and more fun when you know you have the correct equipment to hand.

HAND TOOLS

TAPE MEASURE - This is probably the most important tool in your kit. Keep it clean and free from damage at all times.

PENCIL - I'm sure in my lifetime I have purchased thousands of pencils and on every project I lose them! Keep it safe and keep it sharp.

SCRIBE - If you are marking something accurately a pencil line can sometimes be too thick. Use a scribe or even a sharp screw or nail to scratch the mark.

HAMMER - These vary in price and quality but it's worth investing in a decent one. I have a beautiful hammer with a leather handle that I refuse to use for hitting things with!

SCREWDRIVERS - It's worth having a basic set of screwdrivers, but the main one you will use is a PZ2, a medium-sized cross head that fits most screws. Traditional furniture is sometimes held together using flat-head screws, which are great to look at when all the slots line up neatly, but are very easy to slip off compared with a cross head. A Phillips is a four-pointed cross head, while a Pozi has eight points of contact.

CLAMPS - Whether an old-fashioned metal G clamp or a modern quick-release plastic clamp, you need a couple of these — they make life easier and safer.

HACKSAW - A compact saw that's great for quickly cutting small items such as plastic pipe or a metal bar.

COPING SAW - The fine blade allows you to cut out intricate shapes with ease. It has a clever deep-framed design to avoid hitting the material.

PANEL SAW - A fancy name for a big wood saw. Slightly tricky to use at first, but great for cutting straight lines. Remember to use the handle as a square to get your 45- and 90-degree angles.

SANDPAPER - Comes in a variety of grits, from really rough 40 grit to very fine wet and dry. Work up through the grades for best results. Wrapping the paper around a sanding block of wood helps.

FILES - Used on plastic or metal, these come in all shapes and styles. Flat files sand a straight edge, half-moon files have one flat and one contoured surface, and a round file is ideal for finishing inside metal pipework.

SPANNERS - I do carry an adjustable spanner (wrench) in my toolbox, but I try to use proper spanners when possible. Standard spanners are great, but I love a ratchet spanner; it's handy in limited spaces and saves your knuckles being bashed.

SOCKET SET - This carries out the same job as a spanner in terms of tightening and loosening nuts and bolts, but is easier to use in tight locations.

ALLEN KEYS - A small set of Allen keys (hex wrenches) will be really useful, particularly with bicycles.

CHISEL - Used when shaping wood, a sharp set of chisels is very handy. They take some practice to use properly, but once mastered they make it possible to create some beautiful joints in timber.

BOLSTER - A bigger industrial chisel, used on masonry to chip away concrete, and similar building materials.

RUBBER MALLET - Ideal for use when assembling delicate materials you don't want to mark. Alternatively, you can sometimes use a hammer with a spare block of soft wood between it and the surface you are hitting.

CLUB HAMMER - A small heavy hammer, usually used with a bolster.

POWER TOOLS

CORDLESS DRILL — Can be used for drilling holes and inserting screws. You can buy polishing and sanding heads, and cone cutters for larger holes.

PILLAR DRILL - Basically a drill that is mounted on a vertical pole to keep it upright — much easier when trying to drill accurate holes, as you can also clamp the material.

POCKET HOLE JIG - New to my workshop last year after I saw a carpenter using one, this clamps wood to enable you to drill a diagonal hidden hole, which allows for hidden screw fixings.

IMPACT DRIVER - Basically similar to a cordless drill, but rattles as you are inserting screws to drive them deep quicker. It's not great for fine work and doesn't have a torque setting like a drill driver, but fantastic for large construction that will be covered up.

MITRE SAW — A spinning circular blade used to cut lengths of wood; most cut in at least one angle but some cut in two.

SMALL VIBRATING MOUSE SANDER — Affordable and easy to use, this is great for getting into intricate detailing.

ORBITAL SANDER — This removes material a lot quicker, but is less controllable.

BELT SANDER — The most aggressive sander, this removes the most material quickly but is the least delicate.

WELDER — A little more specialist and requires decent safety equipment, but it basically joins metal together without the need for fixings. Equipment can be expensive and takes a bit of practice, but is very satisfying once mastered.

RIVET GUN — A very simple way of joining two pieces of flat material is to drill a hole through both pieces, place a rivet in the hole and pull the trigger.

JIGSAW — Great for cutting out intricate shapes, this can be used on most materials with the appropriate blade. It's not great for cutting straight lines unless you use a guide.

ANGLE GRINDER — Generally used for cutting, sanding or polishing metal. The thin blade, for example, is great at cutting cast-iron bathtubs, the sanding disc is good for sanding back the cut edges of a shopping trolley (cart), and the polishing pad for making aeroplane wings really shine.

TABLE SAW — A circular blade protruding up through a table or bench — great for cutting large, flat sheets of wood.

CIRCULAR SAW — A hand-held circular blade, similar to a table saw, this is perfect for cutting straight lines but is not good for curves or details.

BLOW TORCH - This tool is traditionally used for joining copper plumbing pipework, but recently I've been using mine for charring wood (see page 86).

TRICKS AND TECHNIQUES WHEN UPCYCLING OUTDOORS

There are some skills you simply learn over time, that come with experience. I can try to give you as many tips as possible, but the best way to learn is by rolling up your sleeves and having a go. It's sometimes hard to get started when you are working with a new item or material, but don't be afraid to get stuck in. Remember, we all make mistakes — just try to learn from them!

For example, the first time I cut up a shopping trolley (cart) it sprung open under tension, which I wasn't expecting. It stabbed me in the hand then collapsed when I sat on it! But I'll know next time and treat this type of construction with more caution.

Often when you're designing and experimenting, you are venturing into new territory. The sales assistant at the hardware shop doesn't have an item in stock specifically designed to attach a pallet to a copper pipe, so you'll have to find a work. That's all part of the fun, problem-solving as you go.

SALVAGING WOOD

There are lots of different types of wood available to the eagle-eyed scavenger. Pallets are available from most industrial estates as most businesses receive their deliveries on them and have no way of getting rid of them. If you ask nicely the business owner will generally encourage you to take them.

Plywood is also a fairly common timber — to find decent offcuts check skips (dumpsters), building sites and your local dump. A lot of old furniture was made of solid timber and even modern pine furniture is great to work with.

I've even come to embrace chipboard, recently. This is a wood I have in the past tried to avoid as it's not nice to work with, doesn't give a great finish on the edges and contains lots of glue, which isn't great for respiratory issues. But you have to be open to new ideas and all materials can have their place in certain projects.

Old telephone poles (utility poles) can be useful, as are scaffold boards, although both of these are becoming more sought after and hence slightly more expensive. Railway sleepers (railroad ties) are gorgeous great lumps of timber but beware any nasty chemicals they might have been treated with.

Always think about not only which wood looks best for the project but also what strength you require. Plywood, for example, is extremely strong when used end on, but it is quite flexible down its length. Scaffold boards are usually made from wood that is force grown and hence can twist and split a bit when worked. Sometimes, of course, these attributes can lend themselves to your design, such as the ability to steam-bend plywood to give curved shapes.

SAWING

There are hundreds of different saw styles, but one top tip - go slowly and don't press too hard!

Whether you are using a high-powered circular saw or a junior hacksaw, let the saw do the work. Always use the correct blades for the material you are using and remember when you apply lots of friction to a material you will get flying debris, sharp edges and heat!

HAND SAWS - The blade is usually directional. The teeth cut more when you push and less when you pull. To get started, pull the saw gently a couple of times to create a small groove, then you can start gently pushing forward. Try not to limit yourself to the centre of the blade; long slow strokes using the entire blade will make sawing easier and prolong the life of your blade.

MACHINE SAWS - Whether a circular spinning blade, reciprocating blade or a continuous band, these saws cut fingers off! Treat them with respect, however, and they are your best friend and will save you hours and create more accurate cuts. When possible try to clamp down anything you are cutting, follow safety instructions and, as with hand sawing, take your time and don't push it.

NEW TECHNIQUES I'VE BEEN EXPERIMENTING WITH

CHARRING — This is a Japanese technique to make timber both waterproof and beautiful without using chemicals.

Basically by applying a naked flame to timber it chars the surface, bringing out the grain to create a gorgeous rustic look. This process also makes the timber water-repellent and more resistant to mould and fungus. It is traditionally used on siding on houses.

JAPANESE SAWING - Another tool I've been experimenting with recently is the Japanese pull saw. Its small, thin, flexible blade allows you to cut flush to a flat surface, to trim dowels and such like. As the name suggests the saw only cuts when you pull it, rather than push. This gives the user more control, and a radius on the corners prevents it scratching the surface.

3D PRINTING — Once the exclusive realm of large corporations and limited to prototyping, three-dimensional printing is now very affordable and actually a very useful tool for upcyclers. Imagine finding a stunning old chest of drawers only to find one of the knobs or handles missing, and not being able to find a replacement anywhere. Well, with 3D printing you could simply place one of the other handles into your machine, scan the product then print an exact copy. Less expensive 3D printers only print in plastics, which might be adequate for the job, but if you are after something more structural you can now even print in metal. An alternative is to use the plastic print as a mould from which you can form a new handle using a more traditional manufacturing technique, such as casting.

SHORTCUTS AND TOP TIPS

CHANGING COMPONENT BLADES Switching between blades, discs and drill bits can be a worrying job. To ensure accidents are less likely I always make sure that I disconnect the tool from its power supply. Whether it's a case of removing the battery from a drill or pulling the plug from a socket (wall outlet) on my angle grinder, I only change the dangerous bits when I have clear sight that the power supply is disconnected.

EXTENSION LEADS Be careful when using extension leads as they can overheat very quickly if you use them while they are wound up. It's very tempting to

just unreel the couple of metres (feet) you require for the job you're doing, but you really should unwind the entire cable. First and foremost this is an important safety issue, but there's also a cost factor — do you want to splash out on a new cable to replace the one that's just burned out?

SUPPORTING YOUR HANDS I noticed while having my hair cut that my barber rested his fingers on the side of my head while he used the clippers. It made me laugh as that's exactly what I do in the workshop with power tools. If your hands are hovering in mid air it's sometimes tricky to keep still and be consistent with your movements. Supporting your hands by placing them against the material you're working with (in my barber's case my head!) reduces this problem and makes the job easier.

STOP SPLITTING If you drive a screw straight into timber (particularly near the edge) it can split. To prevent this, drill a small pilot hole roughly the same size as the shank of the screw to allow the thread to cut into the wood and get a good grip.

CUTTING OUT A HOLE Drill holes in the internal corners of a section of material, then cut between them to create nice curves — they look great and also prevent the wood splitting. Sharp corners can create weak points.

CONE CUTTERS These useful bits of kit reduce the need for whole sets of drills when working with a restricted toolbox (for example in the garden). They create a smooth hole that doesn't split the back of the material (see me use them on the Toolbox Barbecue, page 70). They are also perfect for de-burring holes in metal, and can countersink screws.

FORSTNER DRILL BITS For years I've used flat drill bits for creating larger diameter holes, but Forstner bits are magical — they produce a much neater hole and can even be steered, to allow for angled hole making.

LAYING CONCRETE AND PLASTERING This is a skill that takes years to master properly, but with the right mix and trowel it's possible for an amateur enthusiast to produce a pretty good finish. Prepare the surface well and spend time getting the consistency just right: too wet and the mix will fall off, too dry and you won't achieve a smooth finish. I deliberately leave a few trowel marks to give texture and depth.

TAKING APART A PALLET Pallets are produced using ring shank nails, which hold really well. To loosen stubborn nails drop the pallet onto each corner to twist the structure, so the nails come free. You can then take the pallet apart more easily using either a hammer and crow (pry) bar or pallet breaker.

MEASURING, CUTTING AND MARKING

Measure twice and cut once is my mantra in the workshop. Taking your time measuring and marking out can save you time and money in mistakes. This is not so important if you're using a material that you have an abundance of, but if you're working with a unique one-off piece of furniture then you don't want to cut it in the wrong place!

With some materials you can get away with undoing mistakes. When working with metal, for instance, you can often weld two pieces back together as if they were never cut. Timber is slightly less forgiving; often it's possible to reconnect two objects, but there is usually some evidence afterwards. Fabric, however, is an entirely different way of working and I'll be honest, when cutting an expensive length of fabric I often measure three times and cut once, as it scares me!

GETTING THE MEASURE

Measuring is easy, right? We learned how to use a ruler at school. Wrong! Mismeasurement is one of the most common mistakes in the workplace and can have gigantic consequences.

THE ESSENTIAL TAPE MEASURE

Tape measures are awesome. Take that bit of metal on the end of the tape. It isn't loose due to shoddy workmanship. The slack allows you to gain a true measurement when you push the metal against a surface (it moves inwards).

SLIDING BEVEL

When you're working with a piece of old furniture you often find things are not as square as they were when originally made. A sliding bevel allows you to transfer an angle from one object to another. Simply loosen the joint, adjust the bevel until it sits flush to the object, tighten the joint again then mark this angle into your new material.

And did you know the angles between a saw blade and its handle give you 45°- and 90°-degree measurements? Useful to know when you are cutting timber.

MAKING YOUR MARK

Marking your measurements is an often overlooked skill. One simple line is all it takes. Depending on the precision required, you may wish to use a scribe, which scratches a very thin line into your material. And always consider the thickness of the saw blade you are using. For example, if you cut a 1m (40 inch) piece of wood in half with a table saw you will end up with two pieces shorter than 50cm (20 inches) due to the material removed by the saw blade.

TAKING THE CUT

When it comes to cutting there are usually a number of different ways to do the same job. Use the safest tool for the job that will give accurate well-finished results that require minimal finishing afterwards. Generally speaking, the bigger the blade the straighter the

cut, while thin blades are great for creating intricate shapes.

Try not to be put off with working with the correct material just because it looks hard to cut. Often there will be a simple, safe way of cutting the material that tradespeople are aware of - it just needs a little bit of time investigating and asking the right questions. A prime example of this is cutting copper pipe: you don't need expensive plasma cutters or angle grinders. All you need is a basic pipe slice, which can be picked up cheaply at a hardware store. Clip the slice onto your pipe, give it a few turns and hey presto, you have a perfectly straight cut that doesn't need sanding afterwards.

FINISHES, VARNISHES AND WEATHERPROOFING

As we are focusing on upcycling outdoors, perhaps one of the greatest challenges is treating the materials we use to make sure they don't get destroyed by exposure to the elements.

In the past, treating outdoor timber typically meant staining it sludge brown with an outdoor wood preservative that sealed the timber. Times have changed and now we have a great selection of finishes that allow you to create your desired style, while still nourishing and sealing the material.

WOOD TREATMENTS

OILS — These absorb into wood and nourish it. They need to be reapplied occasionally when the wood looks dry. Some oils add a hint of colour and bring out the grain while others are almost transparent.

WAXES — These are a quick and easy way to treat wood. Various tones of brown and even coloured waxes are available, which give a washed effect that allows you to see the natural grain more than painting. Easy to apply with a cloth or brush, they dry almost instantly.

EXTERIOR CHALK PAINT — Until relatively recently chalk paint was designed to be used only indoors. Now, however, there is an ever-growing range of exterior chalk paint that is UV- and water-resistant. This is perfect when trying to achieve a rustic, aged effect that a gloss paint wouldn't give.

CHARRING — As previously mentioned, treating the surface of wood with a naked flame not only looks great but also makes it water-repellent. This technique is useful for soft wood such as pine.

CRACKLE GLAZE — This product can be used to achieve an authentic aged look when painting furniture. I like to paint a base coat onto the item first. Once this has dried, apply a layer of the crackle glaze. Once dry, apply a generous coat of a contrasting colour. The crackle glaze sucks the moisture out of the paint, which gives it that beautiful effect.

Of course, if you're feeling brave you can always leave materials untreated. I have allowed the scaffold boards on the decking of my houseboat to silver in the sunlight, and I'm actually enjoying the natural bowing and splitting of the wood — it adds character.

METAL

This can be painted in a similar way to wood, spray painted with specialist metal paint or even powder coated — the colour is applied as a powder, while an electric current runs through the metal object, giving a very durable finish.

FIXING AND JOINING

For many years I wasn't a fan of glue. I preferred where possible to use mechanical fixings, such as nuts, bolts and screws. However, having worked with some incredible craftsmen over the last few years, I've learned that there is indeed a time and a place for glue!

I don't think it's always an alternative to a good solid fixing, but as an additional bond between two surfaces that are also screwed, or even between two materials that cannot be drilled or screwed, modern adhesives can be incredibly effective.

Hiding fixings is always a big part of constructing designs. It's one thing drawing a design so that it looks pretty in a picture, but fabricating it in such a way that it's easy to assemble yet hides the fixings can be tricky. Alternatively, sometimes it's lovely to celebrate and enjoy being able to see the honesty of the fixings in all their glory. Aeroplane wings, for example, look glorious with all their rivets proudly on display.

There are loads of great fixing and joining methods available these days, from screws and bolts to rivets and biscuit joints. That doesn't mean we should rule out some of the more traditional methods, such as twine, leather belts and buckles and wire. These materials not only function well; they also add a traditional aesthetic and have an emotional reference to a more simple time.

NUTS & BOLTS

Nuts, bolts, two-part resins, Phillips, Pozi, flat-head screws — the terminology is endless so here is a quick insight into each and how they can be used.

BOLTS are the long thin bits, nuts are the smaller fatter bits that thread onto the bolt — so many people still get this confused! They come in basic metric or imperial sizes — an 8mm diameter bolt is called an M8. You then specify the length in mm. As standard, bolts have a hexagonal-shaped head that is tightened using either spanners or socket sets. The pitch refers to the distance between each thread. The majority of threads are standard pitch, but you occasionally find fine-pitch threads on items such as electrical lighting and spark plugs.

NUTS are the smaller hexagonal bits that thread onto the bolt. They are usually just described by the M number as outlined above. You usually fit a washer to a bolt before the nut to ensure it spins on the washer rather than scratching the surface of the material. If you want a nut to stay fixed for a long time, use a nut with a nylon sleeve or tighten two nuts against each other.

HEX HEAD is the standard bolt head shape.

BUTTON-HEAD BOLTS have a much prettier domed head with a recessed small hexagonal hole into which you place an Allen key (hex wrench) to tighten. They are similar to standard bolts, but more ornate and more expensive. You cannot achieve quite the same level of tightness or torque with these compared with standard hex-head bolts.

COACH BOLTS have a domed head but no recess; this may appear strange as it looks like it's impossible to hold the head as you tighten and slacken the bolt. The secret is a square shank directly under the head which, as you tighten, digs in, stopping it from spinning as you tighten.

NYLOCK NUTS are standard-looking hexagonal nuts but with a nylon insert that binds to the thread as you tighten it. They are used when you don't want the thread to be removed or work loose.

DOMED NUTS work like a standard nut but they have a domed top rather than a flat one so they can only be used on the end of a thread. They are more ornate, designed to be on view, and give increased safety as the bolt thread or sharp end is not exposed.

WASHERS are generally placed between the bolt head and the surface as well as the nut and the surface. These simple rings, which prevent the nut or bolt head scratching the surface, can be a variety of materials, but typically are metal, rubber, nylon or cork.

ACKNOWLEDGEMENTS

As always, I would like to thank my publishers for allowing me to rant in public. Brent Darby's beautiful photography makes everything I produce and every face I pull much more bearable. Debbie and Danielle at Fresh Partners — I can only assume you are carrying out community service for a crime you committed in a past life!

I would like to thank anyone who has put up with me over the last 40 years, from my mum to teachers, rugby coaches, scout leaders, work colleagues, friends and family. I must be a pain to know, let alone love. I am a whirlwind of excitement and ideas, I am always chasing the next big dream and I'm always late. I apologize and thank you, and hopefully I make you smile sometimes.

I am truly blessed and still can't believe a short lad from Bedfordshire has been given these opportunities and an amazing group of people who love and support me as you all do. If you are a young person reading this, currently making important career decisions, then don't panic. Nobody really knows what they are doing or where they are going. Just do everything with passion and enthusiasm to the best of your ability, and the rest will fall into place.

Finally, if you have followed my random journey, watched one of my shows, read a column or bought this book — I hope you enjoy it, and thank you for your continued support.

While writing this book I have been saddened by the passing of my old teacher Mrs Bishop. She was a beautiful, feisty 5ft blonde who for some reason decided I was worth investing time into. She would very rarely shout, but didn't need to — a quick look would give you a telling-off more intense than any raised voices. We had kept in touch since I left school, and she would tell me how proud she was that I'd found my calling. I cannot thank her enough for giving me the confidence and self-belief to fulfill my dreams. Teaching was clearly her calling and through it she educated and influenced so many.

Mrs Bishop — this book is dedicated to you, your family and all those teachers out there, inspiring the next generation.

The publisher would like to thank the following for help with special photography: Gemma Lane and Annabel Adams for making things run smoothly; Isabella Cross and Emma Lambert for modelling; Nigel Martin and Jay Cross for help with construction; The Barn at Glebe Farm Sharnbrook, Bedfordshire, MK44 (an events venue with beautiful gardens and 'The View') and the Lamberts for locations.